DISCOVER SERIES
BUTTERFLY

MARIPOSA

Archiearis Parthenias

Archiearis parthenias

Archon Apollinus

Archon apollinus

Battus polydamas

Battus polydamas

Morpho azul

Blue morpho

Callosamia angulifera

Callosamia angulifera

Catocala sponsa

Catocala sponsa

Arco de chryso

Chryxus arctic

Colias erate

Colias erate

Danaus plexippus

Danaus plexippus

Limenitis arthemis Astyanax

Limenitis arthemis astyanax

Liminitis bredowii

Limenitis bredowii

Liminitis lorquini

Limenitis lorquini

Nymphalis milberti

Nymphalis milberti

Papilio glaucus

Papilio glaucus

Papilio machaon

Papilio machaon

Papilio polyxenes

Papilio polyxenes

Parnissius phoebus

Parnassius phoebus

Phragmatobia luctifera

Phragmatobia luctifera

Pieris brassicae

Pieris brassicae

Pyrrhia umbra

Pyrrhia umbra

Vanessa cardui

Vanessa cardui

Watsonarctia casta

Watsonarctia casta

Zerynthia polyxena

Zerynthia polyxena

Make Sure to Check Out the Other Discover Series Books from Xist Publishing:

   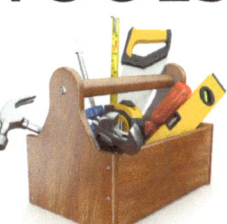    

Published in the United States by Xist Publishing
www.xistpublishing.com
PO Box 61593 Irvine, CA 92602

© 2017 First Bilingual Edition by Xist Publishing
Spanish Translation by Victor Santana
All rights reserved
No portion of this book may be reproduced without express permission of the publisher
All images licensed from Fotolia

ISBN: 978-1-53240-248-7 EISBN: 978-1-53240-249-4

xist Publishing

www.ingramcontent.com/pod-product-compliance
Lightning Source LLC
LaVergne TN
LVHW071031070426
835507LV00002B/110